ANIMALS IN THE CITY

Coyotes

Ava Podmorow

Explore other books at:
WWW.ENGAGEBOOKS.COM

VANCOUVER, B.C.

↱ WWW.ENGAGEBOOKS.COM

Coyotes: Level Pre-1
Animals in the City
Podmorow, Ava 2004 –
Text © 2022 Engage Books
Design © 2022 Engage Books

Edited by: A.R. Roumanis
and Sarah Harvey

Text set in Epilogue

FIRST EDITION / FIRST PRINTING

LIBRARY AND ARCHIVES CANADA CATALOGUING IN PUBLICATION

Title: Coyotes / Ava Podmorow.
Names: Podmorow, Ava, author.
Description: Series statement: Animals in the city
Engaging readers: level pre-1, beginner.

Identifiers: Canadiana (print) 20220396361 | Canadiana (ebook) 2022039637X
ISBN 978-1-77476-744-3 (hardcover)
ISBN 978-1-77476-745-0 (softcover)
ISBN 978-1-77476-746-7 (epub)
ISBN 978-1-77476-747-4 (pdf)

Subjects:
LCSH: Readers (Elementary)
LCSH: Readers—Coyote.
LCGFT: Readers (Publications)

Classification: LCC PE1119.2 .P632 2022 | DDC J428.6/2—DC23

This project has been made possible in part
by the Government of Canada.

Canada

Coyotes are
very bold!

3

Coyotes come to cities from deserts and mountains.

They are looking for food, shelter, and safety.

They like to eat fruits, vegetables, rats, and mice.

Coyotes will also eat human garbage. It can make them sick.

Coyotes have slim bodies and bushy tails.

Bushy Tail

Yellow Eyes

Their eyes are yellow.

Coyotes can be gray, white, beige or brown.

Coyote babies are born in holes called dens.

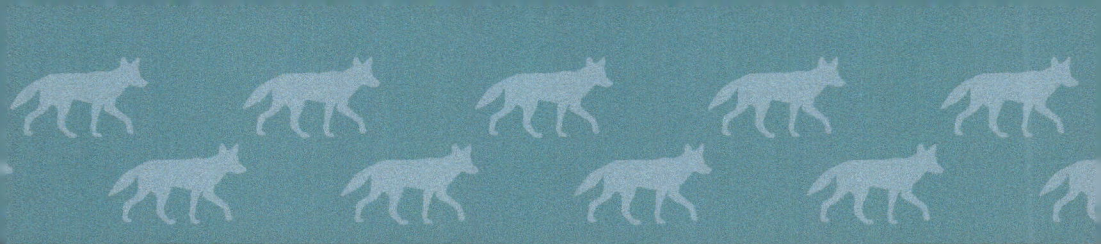

Baby coyotes are called pups.

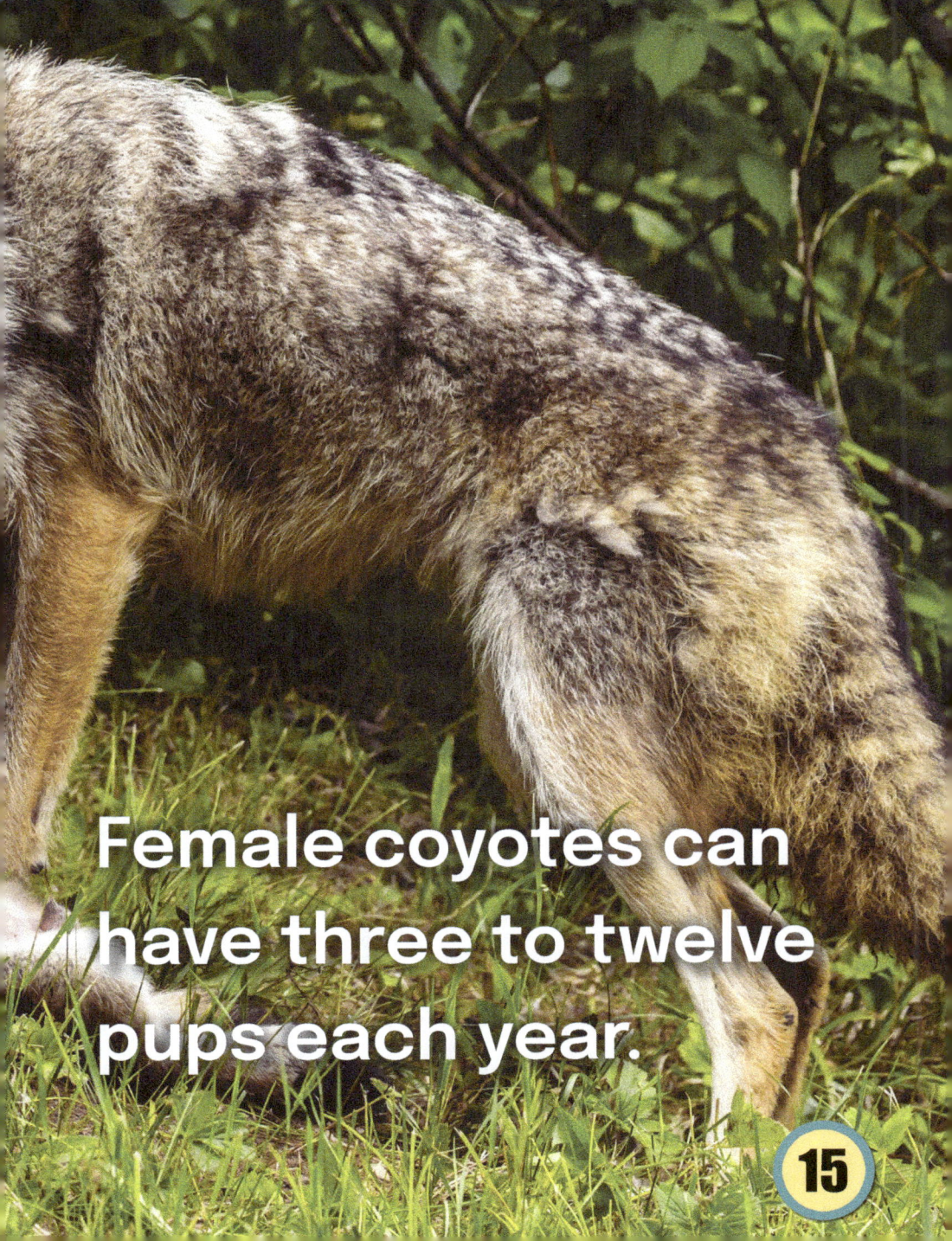

Female coyotes can have three to twelve pups each year.

Pups live in dens
for about a month.

Once they come out of the den they are ready to be on their own.

Coyotes sleep
during the day.

They hunt at night, when they can see better.

Coyotes can hear noises from far away.

Coyotes are very
fast runners.

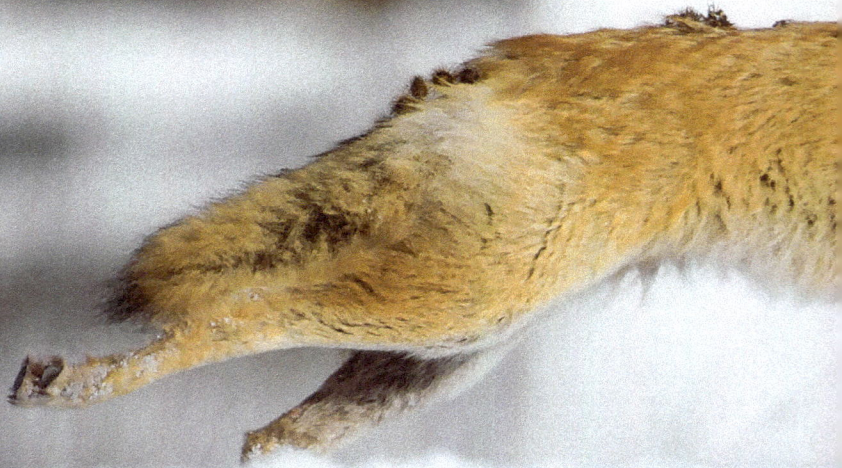

They are also
good swimmers.

Coyotes can make 11 different noises.

Coyotes howl to keep people and animals away.

They bark when
they are in danger.

Thanks for keeping your city clean.

Explore other books in the Animals In The City series.

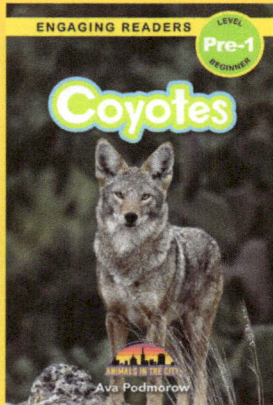

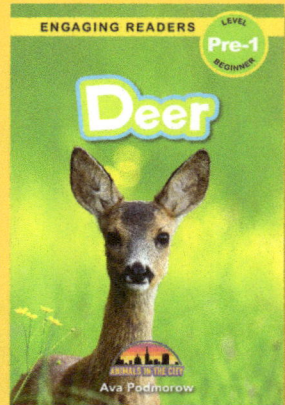

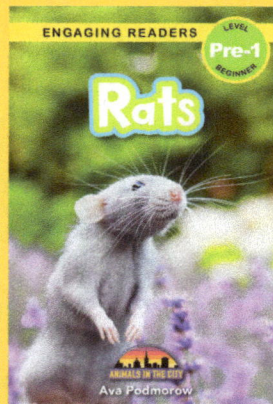

Visit www.engagebooks.com/readers

Explore level 1 readers with the Animals That Make a Difference series.

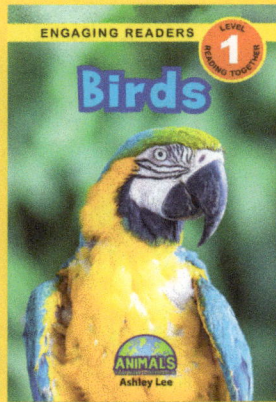

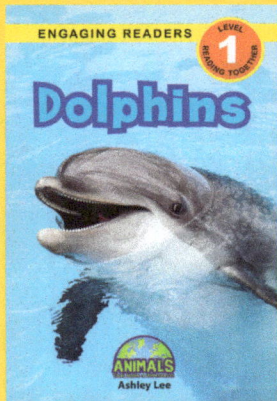

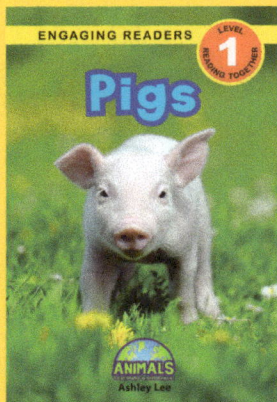

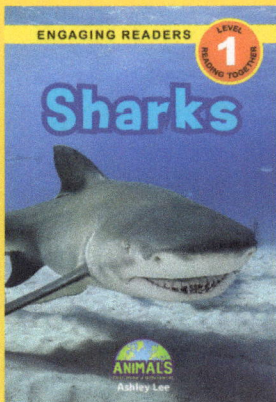

Visit www.engagebooks.com/readers

www.ingramcontent.com/pod-product-compliance
Lightning Source LLC
Chambersburg PA
CBHW051235020426
42331CB00016B/3390